THERE'S A WAY BACK TO GOD

by

WILLIAM MACDONALD

WALTERICK PUBLISHERS
P. O. Box 2216
Kansas City, Kansas

Printed in U.S.A.

TABLE OF CONTENTS

THERE'S A WAY BACK TO GOD

WHAT HAPPENED TO BUD?

Before Bud became a Christian, he had been a drinking, swearing sailor. If you had told him that he would ever be "religious," he would have laughed at you—and probably cursed. He tried hard to impress his shipmates with his capacity for liquor and his wolfish love life. He was a swaggering, swinging swabbie.

However, there was at least one seaman on the aircraft carrier who wasn't impressed. Chuck was the leader of a Bible class that met weekly in one of the store-rooms. He and Bud had been at Boot Camp together. Chuck had spoken to Bud periodically about his fouled-up life and his need of Christ. The response had been hostile at first, then Bud pretended to be disinterested. Chuck was patient—and persistent.

Bud would never attend the Bible class, of course; that would have marred the image he had worked so hard to create. But once or twice, in brief encounters with Chuck, he had asked questions that betrayed an underlying sense of need.

One night when Bud was returning alone to the ship after an evening of drinking in Honolulu, he was attacked by three thugs, beaten, robbed and left unconscious in an alley. The Shore Patrol found him and took him to the ship where he spent two days in the sick bay.

Not long after that, Chuck happened to stand next to Bud in the chow line. They ate supper together, then walked back to the storeroom for a talk. Bud was ready. Chuck presented the Good News of salvation, then challenged him to make a complete commitment of his life to the Lord Jesus Christ.

Utterly broken, Bud knelt beside a row of boxes and said, "God, I've been in a blackout up till now, but now I see the Light."

His life was transformed. All the false bravado was gone. He broke with several unclean habits almost immediately. He began attending the Bible class. There he learned to have a daily quiet time. He also started a systematic program of Scripture memory. And he began to witness to his buddies.

At first the ridicule was hard to take, especially when a crowd of fellows was standing around. "The 'red devil' had become a 'deacon,'" they quipped. Bud usually said nothing to the crowd, but talked to the fellows individually about the Lord when he had the chance.

After a few weeks, the jeering subsided. The change in his life, his consistent testimony and his loving, outgoing manner in witnessing to others won him a certain measure of respect.

During the remainder of his hitch in the Navy, Bud continued to grow spiritually. He succeeded Chuck as leader of the Bible class when Chuck was transferred to another carrier. Through Bud's witness and teaching, thirty-five men on the ship professed faith in the Lord Jesus.

That was over six years ago. Bud is now a civilian, living in Homestead, Arizona. He is married and has two children—a son and a daughter. He is a salesman for a national air-conditioning company.

But he is no longer "on fire" for the Lord. Fact is he never goes near a church. Neither does his wife. And the children have never been to Sunday School. Bud has no Christian friends; in fact, he seems to avoid the Christians as much as possible.

Two weeks ago, Chuck was going home to Texas on leave. He stopped off in Homestead to visit Bud (he had heard that things weren't going too well).

When Chuck pulled up in front of the house, Bud was at the side, working on his car. They greeted each other cordially enough, but something was missing. There was a sense of restraint. The old openness was gone.

After about ten minutes, Chuck decided to break through the barrier.

"Whatever has happened to you, Bud?"

Bud didn't reply—just ground his cigarette into the gravel driveway with his foot.

Chuck tried again: "Bud, no one could ever tell me you weren't saved that night in the store-room."

Bud glanced toward the house to see if anyone might be listening. Then he said, "Sure, I was saved . . . but I'm away from the Lord." There was a pathos about him as he shifted nervously against the front right fender of his car.

"Sure, I was saved, but I'm away from the Lord!"

"Saved, but away from the Lord!"

What happened to Bud?

How did he get away from the Lord?

Can he come back?

How?

FELLOWSHIP IS A TENDER THREAD.

Bud's case is typical of an all-too-common phenomenon in the Christian life—the phenomenon known as backsliding. A backslider is a true believer who is out of fellowship with God because of unconfessed sin in his life.

What do we mean by being out of fellowship with God? Well, it's this way! God is holy and sinless. There is no darkness in Him at all (I John 1:5). In order to walk in fellowship with God, a man must confess and forsake his sins as soon as he is aware of them. After all, fellowship means sharing in common. How can two people get along as partners unless they are agreed? How can a man be in fellowship with God if the man condones sin in his life while God condemns it? (I John 1:6,7).

Fellowship in a human family means that the members are living happily together. But suppose that the husband and wife have a bitter quarrel! The fellowship is broken. A dark cloud of resentment and tension settles down. And the happy family spirit remains broken until the husband and wife confess and make up.

And so it is in the family of God. Sin breaks fellowship. The tender thread of fellowship snaps. And that thread remains broken until the sin is confessed and put away.

But while sin breaks fellowship, it does not break relationship. At the time of conversion, a person becomes a child of God through faith in the Lord Jesus Christ (John 1:12). This relationship is brought about by spiritual birth. Nothing can break it. Once a birth has taken place, the relationship cannot be changed. It is indissoluble.

That is why the believer's relationship has been likened to an unbreakable chain, whereas his fellowship is more like a single strand of a spider's web. When a Christian sins, he is still a child of God, but the happy family spirit is gone.

He does not lose his salvation, but he does lose the joy of his salvation.

It can happen to any believer. In most cases, it begins with neglect of the Word of God and of prayer. The pressures of life eat away at the daily quiet time. As we get away from the influence of the Bible, we no longer take such a serious view of sin. We develop sort of a liberal, indulgent attitude. Temptations no longer seem repulsive; in fact, the anticipation of sin becomes attractive. We rather enjoy thinking about it—not that we would ever do it, of course. But we think about it so much that it becomes rather familiar to us. Then we dabble, we trifle, we sample—and finally we plunge (James 1:14,15).

Most believers backslide at one time or another in their lives. The Bible tells us about some outstanding saints who allowed sin to break communion with God—Lot, Samson, Naomi, David, Jonah, Peter and Demas, for instance. The Christian who thinks it couldn't happen to him is in greatest danger of a tumble (I Cor. 10:12).

As soon as the thread of fellowship is broken, the Holy Spirit goes to work to bring about our restoration. He seeks to convict us of sin and bring us to the place of repentance and confession. Because of our pride and hardness, this may take weeks, months or even years.

All sin must be confessed to God. But if others have been affectetd by our sin it must be confessed to them as well (Matt. 5:23,24). And restitution must be made in all cases where our sin has caused tangible loss to others.

As soon as there has been genuine confession Godward and manward, and restitution has been made, then fellowship with God is restored, and the Holy Spirit can resume the ministry He loves—occupying the believer with the glories of the Lord Jesus Christ (John 16:14).

Does this mean, then, that a Christian can sin and get away with it? The answer is obviously NO. But in considering the question it is helpful to make a distinction between the PENALTY of sin and the CONSEQUENCES of sin.

It is clear from the Bible that the backslider will never have to pay the eternal penalty of his sin. That penalty was paid by the Savior when He hung on the Cross. Those who believe on Him will not come into judgment, but have already passed from death to life (John 5:24). In other words, when a true believer sins, he is not thereby doomed to hell. Christ made complete satisfaction for sin's penalty by shedding His blood at Calvary. God will not demand payment twice, first from Christ and then from us.

When a child of God sins, the devil accuses him before the Throne of God in heaven. Then the Lord Jesus steps forward as Advocate, points to the wounds in His hands, feet and side, and says, in effect, "I paid for that sin 1900 years ago. Charge it to My account" (I John 2:1).

So the backslider will not have to pay the eternal consequences of his sin in hell. But let us quickly add that he will have to suffer the consequences of his sin in this life and in heaven as well.

Some of the consequences of sin in this life are:

a. Dishonor brought on the Name of the Lord.

b. Ruined testimony.

c. Misery and unhappiness brought on others.

d. Enormous waste of time and money.

e. Physical and emotional disturbances.

f. Deep shame and remorse.

g. Personal misery and wretchedness.

h. Wasted opportunities for serving Christ.

i. Others stumbled by the example of the backslider.

The consequences of sin in heaven include:

a. Loss of reward at the Judgment Seat of Christ (I Cor. 3:15).

b. A reduced capacity for enjoying the Lord and enjoying the glories of heaven.

And yet God is greater than all our sins. He waits for the backslider to return. The door is always open. A royal welcome awaits him. And the Lord has wonderful ways of overruling our sin and failure for His own glory and for our own good.

We have seen then that the cause of all backsliding is sin. It is this that breaks communion with God. And fellowship remains broken until sin in confessed and forsaken.

But now we want to notice that backsliding takes various forms. Though the basic cause is the same and the cure is the same in all cases, yet there are many different manifestations of this spiritual ailment.

FORMS OF BACKSLIDING.

First of all, we might mention the **moral backslider**. This refers to the Christian who falls into sexual sin. Take A——C——, for example. He had been married for fifteen years and had been active in the church. He was an average Christian —with perhaps this one exception. He seemed to be excessively familiar with women. He had a glib tongue, an easy manner, and hands that inclined toward caressing and fondling. It all happened when he was away from home on a business trip. Since then he has been spotty in church attendance. Things have never been the same at home. No one knows what happened. All they know is that he is different —cold—aloof—unresponsive. So far he has kept it all bottled up within himself, and that's the way he intends it to be.

Then there is the **prodigal son type of backslider**. Such as B——- D——. He had been brought up in a sheltered Christian home and was saved the year before he enlisted in the Marines. It was a great relief for him to get away from the restraints of home life. He was determined to "live it up." During his time in the Marines, no one would have known that he was a Christian. He moved along with the crowd and tried to conform as much as possible. All this time he was acting a part. It wasn't the real B—— D—— and he knew it. Deep within there was a sense of guilt and dissatisfaction.

E—— G—— was an **intellectual backslider**. After Bible school he went on to college. He had two good reasons for going. The first was his determination not to be drafted into the Army. The second was his desire for a degree from an accredited college. His major was philosophy. Within the first month his Christian beliefs were severely shaken. He became moody and critical. He lost the simplicity that is in Christ, and became filled with doubts and speculations.

Then, of course, there is the backslider who becomes a **drinker**. With H—— F——, it started as social drinking.

When he took his customers to supper, he joined them by taking a cocktail. But when pressures at home and in business increased, he found escape in drinking more heavily. Now he is in the grip of the habit, but he still feels he can shake it off whenever he wants to. When he thinks of the church and of his Christian friends, he is almost overcome with shame. To find relief, he takes another drink.

Another common type of backslider is a Christian who is married to an unbeliever and who has become discouraged and defeated, **the unequal yoke backslider.** T—— S—— was a radiant Christian girl who shared the Lord with everyone she met. Her fiance professed to be saved after they had been going together three weeks. Today she is sure it was an empty profession. They have little in common. There is constant strife in the home. The children are irritable and rebellious. The husband tells her he doesn't care for her—or for the children. He spends most evenings with his friends. She sits at home, brooding and weeping. She tried to go on for the Lord for a few years after their marriage, but now she has given up.

Then there are **business backsliders.** They may not have committed any gross sins, but they have allowed business to occupy their time so that there is little left for home or for the Lord. They seldom read the Word or pray, and their infrequent attendance at church is a mere formality. The cares of this life have sapped away their spiritual vitality. They are victims of covetousness and materialism.

And there are many others. Some who are disappointed in love, or suffer some great reverse, become cold and carnal. Instead of accepting these things as God's will and as blessings in disguise, they pout and sulk and lose the spiritual glow.

Some have an unforgiving spirit. They have been wronged, and everyone knows it. But they are unwilling to forgive and forget. And so they become vindictive and pharisaical and without mercy. God cannot grant parental forgiveness to believers who are unwilling to forgive one another (Matt. 6:14,15).

Many Christians lapse into a backslidden condition through constant bickering in the home. Some minor disagreement shatters the peace of the household. The walls vibrate with strife. Diplomatic relations between husband and wife are severed. The family altar is discontinued; it would be a farce to pray together when they can't even talk civilly to one another. Neither is willing to give in; they are as unyielding as bars of iron. Each one thinks he is right, not realizing that both are in a backslidden state.

And so we could go on. There are any number of forms in which backsliding can manifest itself. But it all stems from sin—disobedience, immorality, lack of love, unwillingness to forgive, worldliness, covetousness and so forth.

Perhaps it will surprise some to know that true believers can get as far away from the Lord as the cases just cited. Then it may be helpful to remind ourselves that:

1. David was a moral backslider. He committed the sins of adultery and murder (II Sam. 11:1-27).

2. Noah committed the sin of drunkenness after he had been saved through the flood of God's judgment (Gen. 9:20,21).

3. Lot was a business backslider. He sought for prestige and wealth in Sodom (Gen. 13:7-11; 19:1-28).

And these were all restored to fellowship with the Lord. If they could be restored, so can any true believer who has wandered away.

IN THE FAR COUNTRY.

One of the earliest symptoms of spiritual decline is the accumulation of dust on the Bible. It no longer seems important to spend regular time in the Word. What difference does it make if a day is skipped? But soon it is not just a day. Now it is several days, now a week, and now Bible study is abandoned entirely. There is no taste for the Scriptures, no sense of need.

And prayer! It used to form such a vital part of the spiritual life. But somehow the pattern has been broken. The prayer life becomes spotty, then disappears completely. After all, prayer does seem to be rather vague and intangible and mystical, doesn't it?

As far as attendance at the meetings of the local assembly, here too there is a gradual slackening off. The messages are such dull affairs! And so many of the people are religious hypocrites! Perhaps it would be better not to go at all . . . The Christians soon become concerned and try to make contact with him, but the fugitive proves too elusive for them. He is downright uncomfortable in the presence of believers by now.

Increasingly he finds his friendships and his pleasures outside the sphere of the church. At first he seems a trifle awkward to be participating in things that his mother always called "worldly," but soon he has lost his inhibitions and has developed remarkable poise and proficiency.

As he declines spiritually, certain warning voices are raised along the way. People say things that pierce him, although they are not aware of it. In letters, newspaper articles, and on TV, he sees red flags, but he passes on heedlessly.

The joy of his salvation has long since disappeared. He used to be able to talk intelligently and enthusiastically about the Lord Jesus. He couldn't do it now, at least not the enthusiastic bit. He used to sing too . . . the songs of an effervescent Christian. Actually, he still sings occasionally, but not out of the same book.

He has developed a critical attitude toward life in general. Perhaps this is because nothing ever goes right for him. He seems to get all the bad breaks. If only things would click for awhile . . . but they don't. And so he takes it out on others. Whereas once he was affable and kindly, now he is hard and sullen.

At first, he must jump a high hurdle before he can commit a new sin. But after that, his defenses are down and it never seems so hard again. Then he decides he might as well go all the way.

To justify himself, he goes through quite a complicated series of rationalizations. Strangely enough he can even find Scripture verses that support him in his current manner of life. And he reasons that plenty of sanctimonious Christians do things that are a lot worse than he does. And the trouble with most Christians is that they're too legalistic. And his parents were far too strict with him when he was a kid.

By the time he gets through, he is saying that certain sins are not sin because they are done in love. He is proving that black is white.

The truth is he's miserable. He knows too much to be happy, living like this. But he would never admit it. He is a good actor, and can put on a carefree front. The last thing he'd want to do is break down and confess his inward wretchedness.

He is constantly leading a double life, always trying to cover up. And there is the nagging fear of being exposed. Perhaps he even resorts to bribes or "hush money" to protect himself.

Sometime he is surprised at the disgusting situations in which he finds himself. He tolerates conditions now that he would have howled against at home. He realizes that his poorest Christian friends are better off then he. But he seems to be trapped—and he endures it meekly.

In the area of speech he has changed most noticeably. It must be pretty bad when some of his ungodly friends rebuke him: "You used to talk decently when you first came here, but listen to you now." It hurts deeply to take abuse from such dissolute profligates.

And that isn't all that hurts! There is the matter of wasted opportunities for witnessing. He sees so many of his friends in deep spiritual need, but what can he say? Some even come to him and ask questions that leave the door wide open to speak for the Lord. But his lips are sealed. Once or twice he did try feebly to give a little spiritual help, but someone said, "If you believe that, what are you doing here?" After that, he decided it would be better to say nothing.

Perhaps the most shocking part of it all is that at least once he has stooped to depths to which unbelievers seldom go. He is stunned when he thinks of it now. Often he would like to talk to someone about it, but no one would understand. So he keeps it all bottled up within himself.

And he is amazed at how love turns to hatred. Now as he thinks of his partner in sin, he hates that partner with a hatred as deep as the love that formerly he professed (II Sam. 13:15).

Life seems to have turned into a treadmill. He works harder than ever but never seems to get anywhere. The money leaks out of his hands and pockets. Unusual expenses arise, like the auto repairs after the accident. And the freak electrical fire in the apartment.

And also his medical bills have been high. He has been making frequent trips to the doctors, and has been through a battery of tests. So far they haven't found any organic trouble. But the pain is still there, and the other symptoms.

He lives in hope that soon his circumstances will change. Things can't always be as bad as this. Maybe if B----- died, that would solve the problem. So he waits for a funeral which never comes. Maybe his own funeral would even solve the problem. He thought of that—even thought of ending it all—but that's as far as he dared to go.

TOUCHING BOTTOM.

Sooner or later, a crisis has to come. If a person is a true believer, he cannot continue away from God indefinitely. There must come a time when he reaches the bottom—the dregs—the husks.

The bottom might be an open grave on a bleak wintry day, where he watches a little white casket lowered into the ground.

The bottom may be an accident in which he miraculously is the only survivor.

It may be a hospital bed where he is left by the hour to think and brood.

Or it may be none of these. It may simply be the end of human endurance. The moment when he abandons all hope of solving his own problems.

You might say it is a time of desperation and utter frustration. Further struggle seems futile. Every escape route is blocked.

THE VOICE THAT WHISPERS "HOPELESS."

Right at that crucial moment, there is a voice that whispers, "It's hopeless."

"There's absolutely no use trying."

"You might as well give up."

"All you can do is cooperate with the inevitable."

"Things could never be the same anyway. The bird with the broken wing never flies as high again."

"You've sinned away your day of opportunity."

"You've passed the point of no return."

"All the king's horses and all the king's men couldn't put Humpty-Dumpty together again."

And the voice goes on echoing down a long empty corridor.

"Hopeless."

"No way out."

"Beyond recall."

"Impossible."

THE VOICE THAT SAYS "COME HOME."

But in that dark, lonely hour there's another Voice, and this Voice is filled with bright promise. It says:

"There is a way back to God."

"The door is always open."

"The past can be forgiven and blotted out. The accumulated guilt of a million sins can be cleansed in a moment."

"There can be a new beginning."

"Things can be as good as they ever were—even better."

"God is able to restore the years that the locusts have eaten."

"No case is too hard for the Lord—not even yours."

"Why don't you come home?"

THE CRITICAL DECISION.

Then comes the great moment of decision. He is torn apart by conflicting emotions. On the one hand there is the scalding shame of admitting sin and failure. On the other is the fierce desire to return home and make things right again.

As soon as he thinks of doing an about-face, a thousand devils seem to pull him back. He wonders that a human body can contain such violent, contrary tensions.

Once more he hears the voice of God—not harsh and vindictive but tender and loving:

"Return ... to the Lord your God, for you have stumbled because of your iniquity. Take with you words and return to the Lord; say to Him, 'Take away all iniquity; accept that which is good and we will render the fruit of our lips'" (Hosea 14:1,2, RSV).

Then the moment of great resolve arrives. The dam of built-up tension bursts with a fury. The tears begin to flow, with broken-hearted sobbing. The proud, stiff-necked backslider lies prostrate at the feet of the Savior.

Soon the trembling lips are speaking:

"Have mercy on me, O God, according to thy steadfast love; according to thy abundant mercy blot out my transgressions. Wash me thoroughly from my iniquity, and cleanse me from my sin!

"For I know my transgressions, and my sin is ever before me. Against thee, thee only, have I sinned, and done that which is evil in thy sight, so that thou art justified in thy sentence and blameless in thy judgment. Behold, I was brought forth in iniquity, and in sin did my mother conceive me.

"Behold, thou desirest truth in the inward being; therefore teach me wisdom in my secret heart. Purge me with hyssop, and I shall be clean; wash me, and I shall be whiter than snow. Fill me with joy and gladness; let the bones which thou hast broken rejoice. Hide thy face from my sins, and blot out all my iniquities.

"Create in me a clean heart, O God, and put a new and right spirit within me. Cast me not away from thy presence, and take not thy holy Spirit from me. Restore to me the joy of thy salvation, and uphold me with a willing spirit.

"Then I will teach transgressors thy ways, and sinners will return to thee. Deliver me from bloodguiltiness, O God, thou God of my salvation, and my tongue will sing aloud of thy deliverance.

"O Lord, open thou my lips, and my mouth shall show forth thy praise. For thou hast no delight in sacrifice; were I to give a burnt offering, thou wouldst not be pleased. The sacrifice acceptable to God is a broken spirit; a broken and contrite heart, O God, thou wilt not despise" (Psalm 51:1-17, RSV).

"I have sinned against heaven, and before thee, and am no more worthy to be called thy son; make me as one of thy hired servants" (Luke 15:18b, 19).

Already there is a sensation of tremendous relief. A load has been lifted. A great light has begun to dawn—the dawning of a new day.

The words of the Apostle John come to his mind: "If we confess our sins, he is faithful and just to forgive us our sins, and to cleanse us from all unrighteousness" (I John 1:9). He clings to this promise as if everything depended on it.

Then he remembers how the prodigal son returned and what a royal welcome was waiting for him.

"And he arose, and came to his father. But when he was yet a great way off, his father saw him, and had compassion, and ran, and fell on his neck, and kissed him. And the son said unto him, Father, I have sinned against heaven, and in thy sight, and am no more worthy to be called thy son. But the father said to his servants, Bring forth the best robe, and put it on him; and put a ring on his hand, and shoes on his feet: And bring hither the fatted calf, and kill it; and let us eat, and be merry: For this my son was dead and is alive again; he was lost, and is found. And they began to be merry."

He thinks especially of the words " . . . his father . . . ran, and fell on his neck, and kissed him." He realizes that this is what has happened to him too. The Father saw him when he was still a long way off. He ran and embraced him and kissed him. He understands what the words mean, because he is enjoying the Father's kiss.

The best robe . . .

a ring on his hand . . .

shoes on his feet . . .

and the fatted calf . . .

CALL ME BITTER.

The bells have begun to ring in his soul, but there is still a tremendous hurdle—going back to his Christian family and friends. He recoils at the shame of having to face them. He fears their reaction. Will they be cold and distant? Will they try to avoid him? Or be critical?

He remembers Naomi in the Old Testament. When she returned to Bethlehem after a period of backsliding in Moab, the people asked, "Is this Naomi?"

She answered, "Don't call me Naomi (which means pleasant); call me Mara (meaning bitter); for the Almighty hath dealt very bitterly with me. I went out full, and the Lord hath brought me home again empty" (Ruth 1:19-21).

He thinks to himself, "That's me. Call me bitter. I went out full. The Lord has brought me back empty."

But his fears concerning how his family and friends will receive him are groundless. They give him a marvelous welcome—almost as if he had come back from the dead. They shake his hand warmly, some hug him, and the tears flow rather freely. There are no recriminations; no one says, "I told you so." Everyone is genuinely glad to see him back.

He tries to express his apologies for the dishonor he has brought on the Name of the Lord, for the grief he has caused his family, for the sorrow he has brought to the Christians in the local church. But they interrupt him with assurances of forgiveness, and with expressions of gratitude that their prayers have been answered. He thought they would make him crawl; here they are, treating him with love and mercy.

Every heartbeat says, "It's wonderful! To be back in fellowship with the Lord and with His people. To have the joy of His salvation restored. To experience the Father's kiss."

In fact, it's something like being born again. The thought

steals across his mind, "I wonder if I was ever saved before." But then the question seems an academic one. If he was never saved before, he's saved now, and that's what counts.

The sense of relief is overwhelming. Not to be fighting against the Lord any more! Not to be so proud and unwilling to break! Not to be forever running away!

He can't get over it! The best robe! A ring on his finger! Shoes on his feet! The fatted calf! The merriment that began but never ended! And no elder brother, wishing the lost son hadn't come home!

ASSURANCE OF FORGIVENESS.

It is wonderful to be restored to the Lord. And yet that doesn't mean that there are no problems from then on. Many believers who are brought back to fellowship with God go through terrible times of conviction and doubt and depression; they have difficulty believing that they have actually been forgiven!

Let us examine some of the common difficulties that they face.

1. How can I know that God has forgiven me?

You can know it from the Word of God. He has repeatedly promised to forgive those who confess and forsake their sins. There is nothing in the universe as sure as the promise of God. In order to know that God has forgiven you, you must believe His Word. Listen to these promises:

"He that covereth his sins shall not prosper: but who confesseth and forsaketh them shall have mercy" (Proverbs 28:13).

"I have blotted out, as a thick cloud, thy transgressions, and, as a cloud, thy sins: return unto me; for I have redeemed thee" (Isaiah 44:22).

"Let the wicked forsake his way, and the unrighteous man his thoughts: and let him return unto the Lord, and he will have mercy upon him; and to our God, for he will abundantly pardon" (Isaiah 55:7).

"Come and let us return unto the Lord: for He hath torn, and He will heal us; He hath smitten and He will bind us up" (Hosea 6:1).

"If we confess our sins, He is faithful and just to forgive us our sins, and to cleanse us from all unrighteousness" (I John 1:9).

2. I know He forgave me at the time I was saved, but when I think of the terrible sins I have committed as a believer, it is hard for me to believe that God can forgive me for these. It seems to me I have sinned against tremendous light and privilege!

David committed adultery and murder; yet the Lord forgave him (II Samuel 12:13).

Peter denied the Lord three times; yet the Lord forgave him (John 21:15-23).

God's forgiveness is not limited to the unsaved. He promises to forgive backsliders as well:

"I will heal their backsliding, I will love them freely: for mine anger is turned away from him" (Hosea 14:4).

If God could forgive us when we were His enemies, will He be less forgiving to us now that we are His children?

"For if, when we were enemies, we were reconciled to God by the death of His Son, much more, being reconciled, we shall be saved by His life" (Romans 5:10).

Those who fear that God cannot forgive them are closer to the Lord than they think because God cannot resist a broken spirit (Isa. 57:15). He can resist the proud and unbroken, but He will not despise the man who is truly repentant (Psa. 51:17).

3. Yes, but how often will God forgive? I committed a certain sin and God forgave me. But I have done it several times since then. Surely God cannot forgive indefinitely.

This difficulty is answered indirectly in Matt. 18:21,22:

"Then came Peter to him, and said, Lord, how oft shall my brother sin against me, and I forgive him? till seven times? Jesus saith unto him, I say not unto thee, Until seven times: but, Until seventy times seven."

Here the Lord teaches that we should forgive one another not seven times, but seventy times seven, which is another way of saying indefinitely.

Now if God teaches us to forgive one another indefinitely, how often will He forgive us? The answer is obvious.

This knowledge should not make us careless or encourage us to sin. On the other hand, such marvelous grace is the strongest possible reason why the believer should not sin.

4. The trouble with me is that I don't feel forgiven.

God never intended that assurance of forgiveness should come through feelings. At one moment, you might feel forgiven, but then a little later, you might feel as guilty as ever.

God wants us to *know* that we are forgiven. And so He has based the assurance of forgiveness on the surest thing in the universe—His own Word. His Word, the Bible, says that if we confess our sins, He forgives our sins (I John 1:9).

The important thing is to be forgiven, whether you feel it or not. A person might feel forgiven and yet not be forgiven; in that case, his feelings would deceive him. On the other hand, a person might truly be forgiven and yet not feel it. What difference do his feelings make as long as God has forgiven him?

The repentant backslider can know he is forgiven on the best authority of all—the Word of the Living God.

5. I fear that in getting away from the Lord, I have committed the unpardonable sin.

Backsliding is not the unpardonable sin.

Actually, there are at least three unpardonable sins mentioned in the New Testament, but they can be committed only by unbelievers.

(a) To attribute the miracles of Jesus, performed by the power of the Holy Spirit, to the devil is unforgivable. It is saying that the Holy Spirit is the devil, and therefore it is blasphemy against the Holy Spirit (Matt. 12:22-32).

(b) To profess to be a believer, and then to completely repudiate Christ is a sin for which there is no forgiveness. This is the sin of apostasy mentioned in Hebrews 6:4-6. It is not the same as denying Christ; Peter did that and was restored. This is the wilful sin of treading under foot the Son of God, counting His blood an unholy thing, and doing despite to the Spirit of grace (Hebrews 10:29).

(c) To die in unbelief is unforgivable (John 8:24). This is the sin of refusing to believe on the Lord Jesus Christ, the sin of dying unrepentant and without faith in Him.

One difference between a true believer and one who is not saved is that the former may fall seven times, but he will rise again.

"The steps of a good man are ordered by the Lord: and He delighteth in his way. Though he fall, he shall not be utterly cast down: for the Lord upholdeth him with His hand" (Psa. 37:23,24).

"For a just man falleth seven times, and riseth up again: but the wicked shall fall into mischief" (Proverbs 24:16).

6. I believe that God has forgiven me but I can't forgive myself.

To anyone who has ever backslidden (and is there any believer who hasn't to some extent?) this attitude is quite understandable. We feel our own utter worthlessness and failure so keenly.

And yet the attitude is unreasonable. If God has forgiven, why should I allow myself to be plagued by feelings of guilt?

Faith claims forgiveness as a fact, and forgets the past —except as a healthful warning not to wander away from the Lord again.

THE CONSEQUENCES OF BACKSLIDING.

From what has been said, the idea may arise that a Christian can sin and get away with it. In other words, all he has to do is confess the sin and forsake it. It sounds too easy.

Therefore it is important that we once again distinguish between the **forgiveness** of sin and the **consequences** of sin.

As to forgiveness we have already noticed that there are two kinds—**judicial** and **parental**.

(a) When a person trusts Jesus Christ as Lord and Savior, he receives **judicial** forgiveness of his sins. This means that God, **the Judge** forgives him on the basis of the work of Christ at Calvary (John 3:18a). The believing sinner will never have to pay the penalty of his sins, since the Savior paid it on the Cross (II Cor. 5:21).

(b) When a believer sins, and then confesses hi sins, he receives **parental** forgiveness. This means tha God, **his Father** forgives him and restores him to fel lowship in the family (I John 1:9).

But then we must remember that sin has consequence: and these consequences sometimes continue through life an on into eternity as well. This may be illustrated in the lives of Bible characters.

(a) Abraham married Hagar during a period of backsliding in Egypt (Gen. 16:1-16). Her descendants (the Ishmaelites) have been bitter foes of God's earthly people ever since.

(b) As a result of his backsliding, Lot lost his wife, his sons in law, his testimony, and he nearly lost his life (Genesis 19:14-26). Also he became the father of the Moabites and the Ammonites, cruel foes of the people of Israel (Genesis 19:33-38).

(c) Samson lost his chastity, his freedom, his testimony, his sight and finally his life (Judges 16).

(d) Naomi lost her husband and two sons in death (Ruth 1:3,5).

(e) David was forgiven of his sins but he was required to restore fourfold for the murder of Uriah; subsequently four of his children died:

> (1) The baby born to Bethsheba died (II Sam. 12:19).
>
> (2) Amnon was slain by Absalom (II Sam. 13:28,29).
>
> (3) Absalom was slain by Joab and his men (II Sam. 18:14,15).
>
> (4) Adonijah was slain by Benaiah (I Kings 2:24,25).

God told David that the sword would not depart from his family, and it never did (II Sam. 12:10).

David was not allowed to build the Temple, because of his failure (I Chron. 22:8).

The consequences of his sin continue to this day. By his backsliding, he gave great occasion to the enemies of the Lord to blaspheme (II Samuel 12:14). Atheists today still blaspheme God for calling David a man after His own heart after David had acted so wickedly.

Who can ever measure the consequences of backsliding? The time that is spent out of fellowship with God, for instance. The loss of reward at the Judgment Seat of Christ.

And what of the influence of the backslider on others? How many have been stumbled by his example? How many parents have lived to see their sin repeated in their family? Or to see their children turned away from the Christian faith? What a price to pay for a few moments of sin!

And what of the wasted opportunities? No tears can ever bring them back.

Who can describe the remorse of the backslider? Who can tell of the pangs of conscience? Who knows the defilement of the mind and spirit that reappears during the most sacred moments of life?

All these things remind us that a Christian cannot sin cheaply. It is still true that "the backslider in heart shall be filled with his own ways" (Prov. 14:14). And we know from Scripture and from experience that "Whatsoever a man soweth, that shall he also reap" (Gal. 6:7).

PRESSING ON TOWARD THE MARK.

While it is true that the consequences of sin are costly, it is also true that God is a God of restoration. He longs to see the restored backslider rising above all the failures of the past and living a Spirit-filled life.

How can the Christian do this? How can he be sure that he will not make the same mistake again?

1. The first thing he should do is to have a thorough housecleaning. This may include the burning of books, the disposal of habit-forming items, the destruction of anything that might stimulate evil desires. Even articles of clothing can have lustful associations. Jude says we are to hate the garment spotted by the flesh (Jude 23). To cling to material things that stir up evil desires betrays insincerity in repentance or ignorance concerning one's power to resist temptation.

2. The second thing he should do to keep himself in fellowship is to confess sin constantly. As soon as he is aware of the slightest wrong in his life, he should take it to the Lord, call it by its name, and judge it in His presence (I Cor. 11:31). There must be brokenness to do this, a continual readiness to take sides with God against sin and self.

3. Next there should be a complete surrender of one's will to the Lord (Rom. 12:1,2). This begins as a crisis experience but continues as a moment-by-moment habit. There is strength and security in being yielded to the will of God, whatever it may be. We wander into a danger zone when we assert our own wills.

4. And certainly the believer must read and obey the Scriptures daily (Psa. 119:9,11). In this way, we are warned against pitfalls, are guided positively and are strengthened against oncoming temptation. It is not enough to read the

Word or to hear it. We must be ready to do whatever the Lord says to us (James 1:22). This attitude of profound submission to the Scriptures is indispensable (Isa. 66:2).

5. Prayer too must be a living, vital force in the believer's life (Phil. 4:6,7). Basically prayer is talking to God. It is taking Him into every area of our lives, seeking His guidance, and acknowledging His Lordship. Prayer should include the constant cry, "Lead us not into temptation but deliver us from evil" (Matt. 6:13).

6. Another sanctifying influence in the Christian's life is regular attendance at the meetings of the local assembly (Heb. 10:25). Association with other believers results in edification and strengthening (Prov. 27:17). Also the regular remembrance of the Savior in the Lord's Supper is a powerful deterrent to sin (I Cor. 11: 23-34).

7. The believer should also seek to keep busy for the Lord (Eph. 5:15,16). Temptation is strongest in moments of idleness when the mind is in neutral and the body is overslept. So there is safety in redeeming the time for the Lord, doing what our hands find to do (Eccl. 9:10).

8. It is also important for a believer to put himself in a position where he has to trust the Lord. We are called to live by faith. But this is something that requires deliberate action on our part. The natural thing is to live by sight, to set aside treasures on earth, to build up reserves, to lean on financial props and crutches. The walk of faith means that we are content with food, clothing and a place to live (I Tim. 6:8), that we invest everything above that in the work of the Lord, and that we trust Him for the future.

9. Finally, the Christian who wants to avoid backsliding should walk softly before the Lord all the days of his life (Isa. 38:15). There is no once-for-all solution to the problem of a victorious Christian life. It is a moment-by-moment walk of humble dependence on the Lord (Prov. 3:5,6).